Pieces Of Me

How I Got From There to Here

Riley Josephine

BookLeaf Publishing
India | USA | UK

Made with ❤ on the BookLeaf Publishing Platform
www.bookleafpub.in
www.bookleafpub.com

Dedication

This book is dedicated to,
every well stocked late night gas station aisle.

Preface

This is the story of me and the life I have led up until now. Some of you may think you know what will be written here, but you may instead be surprised to learn you only know half of the story. This is a story of celebration and a story of pain. It is a look at the harshness of growing up, and the lessons learned the hard way, but it is also about the hope and forgiveness that comes after. Mostly, it is about the love that binds a family together.

Acknowledgements

I would like to thank, my first reader, fan, and biggest cheerleader, my mom. The one whose constant support, encouragement, and survival, ensured I would have every opportunity to grow into the person I am today. This book would not have been possible if it weren't for you saying I could do it even when I was sure I could not. I promise this is the first in a series of others that will follow because you can now hold in your hands proof that your belief in me was worth it. I hope one day you are as proud of me as I am of you. I also have to thank my younger sister Kiley and my younger brothers, Winter and Raven, for their love and support every step of the way. There is no way I would have soared this high if I didn't have you all beside me to encourage me, fight with me, challenge me, and defend me. Thank you for not voting to sacrifice me in favor of a different big sister (I'm kidding).

To the teachers who read my poems on the back of tests and tried to proofread my scribbles, thank you. Thank you for showcasing my pieces and never once letting me doubt that becoming a writer was something I could accomplish. Lani, Mrs. Kratz, Ms. O'Brien, and Ms. Watson, you each inspire me to this day and are the very best teachers a girl could have asked for.

1. Story To Tell

I'm unsure how this all plays out
But I've got hope up to my ears
And enough fear to keep my head on my shoulders
The road is long and well-treaded by now
But to me it looks shiny and new
There's a chance I may get lost
Somewhere far up ahead
Where the winding path escapes my current vision
But for that I've got a handful of faith
tucked inside my pocket.
I can't tell yet if I will make it to the place
I have so often imagined this road leads to
Or if I will stop somewhere along the way
But I know either way it will be an adventure
And I'll have a story to tell

2. A Star is Born

I was made in the quiet of the night
My scream broke the silence
and I was welcomed into existence
With laughter and applause
You'll have to forgive me then
For my flashy style
And dramatic flare
My need to make everything a production
I was born in the moons spotlight
Ready to outshine the stars

3. Like My Mother

People say I look just like you
And I've worn that praise like a crown
You are everything that's hard for me
You are grace and beauty personified
While I am still a gawky fawn struggling to walk
You are gentle when the world rages at you
While I rage right back with fists and anger
You stand up for every injustice
no matter the oppositions strength
While their strength makes my voice tremble
You teach with a firm patience
No matter how often I try to give up
You push me to explore and dare me to be bold
But your hands are always open
When I want to come home
I hope one day
I make you as proud to call me daughter
As I am to call you mom

4. Father's Shoulders

The world looked so small from my perch
Up on my father's shoulders
He carried me up there every time I asked
When I was scared
Or when my little feet stung from the rocks
I'd raise my arms
and he'd lift me high
It was the safest place on earth

Sometimes he'd make me walk on my own
And no amount of pleading would get him
To lift me up away from the dangerous world
But it was never for forever
He always knew right when to pull me up again
To the safety of his shoulders

I did outgrow his shoulders eventually
But he still carried me in his arms
And when I outgrew those
he held my hand tight

I learned to take risks
And be bolder than my brothers
Because I knew my father would be waiting

To help pull me out if I ever got stuck

I dread the day he lets me go for the last time
When no amount of danger
Or pleading will allow him to pick me up
And carry me till it's safe

5. Home Sweet Home

I can remember every house I've lived in
All twenty-two of them
The old, white farmhouse
I took my first steps in
The apartment in the barn
my parents built together
Then the house with merry go round wallpaper
and a snapping turtle in the back
Next came the motor home
we packed our lives into to head out east
The next few are a little bit of a blu
There was the summer I spent
in a tack room at Rockingham Park
Which was before the house
across from the Meadowlands
with the tiny yard
but after the apartment in Monticello
with the porcupine and the dance floor
There was the barn with
one hundred and nine acres of farmland
The house on top of the hill
and the one on the bottom
Then there was the year we spent
in a Hampton Inn motel

The multiple times we've had to live
in our car or hidden in a shed
The two-story farmhouse in
upstate New York
I was sure would be my last stop
There's more I've forgotten
lost to the vast expense of highways
and dirt roads that separate me from them
Sometimes I wonder who lives in the places
I once called home
If they're just passing by like I was
or if they've made those walls the home I never could

6. Little Bugs

The first costume my mother bought me
Was a bright red ladybug with
two black antennas attached to a headband
and a pair of little black shoes
I was the talk of the town
Even if I did almost leave my shoes on a bench

When my sister came
she got to wear the ladybug costume
and I was so upset
I hid the pair of little black shoes
My mother didn't seem to notice
She just gave her my dance shoes to wear

When my little brother came
He too got to wear the ladybug costume
Although my sister had bent one antenna
And his feet barley fit into my old dance shoes
I was less annoyed this time

Finally my baby brother came
And got to put on the ladybug costume
It would be the last time anyone wore it
With its bent antenna

My old dance shoes
And a hole in the seam of the tights
But somehow
He was the cutest one of all of us

That first costume my mother bought for us
Frayed and was given away one day
But it is the reason my mom still calls us
Her baby bugs

7. 2 Am

I once heard that 2am was only
for those who were lonely
or up to no good
But for me

2am was sitting on a couch
wrapped in a blanket
looking out the window
Waiting to see headlights
coming up the drive

2am was for rushing to the door
in Care Bear pj's
and cowgirl boots
to meet my dad

2am was for sleepy hugs
and putting horses away
unloading harnesses
and carrying buckets too big for me

2am was for his laughter
While I talked about my day
And my amazement

While he talked about his night

2am was for old movies I didn't understand
ice cream bowls I didn't deserve
and salty buttery fingers from
scrapping the bottom of a popcorn bowl

2am was for being carried upstairs
back to the bed I should have been in hours ago

2am was a kiss on the forehead
and a goodnight little bug

8. A Little

With each passing day
I grow a little taller and a little stronger
I grow a little bolder and a little smarter
And yet with each passing day I feel this sort of ache
Between the last set of ribs on my left side
It's like a little person is pulling on them
Urging me to stay exactly as I am
It fears something up ahead
Something we may see
Something we may become
It is a silly little person though
We are a roman candle set aflame
When we are finally free
We shall light up the night sky
And nothing will make us afraid
Nothing will put out that light

At least I don't think there is anything...

9. Battlefield

Little bare feet racing through the grass
Unaware of the bombs lying below
Little hands thrown up in celebration
Unaware soon she'll be surrendering in fear
Little girl with a smile so bright
How I wish I could've shielded you from the fight

I watch you now
fear turning to confusion
When it happens for the first time
Words usually laced with love
Dripping with anger and hate
maybe it's just a nightmare

The morning light almost convinces you too
Love graces you again
But I can see it now
Even if you couldn't
The way their hands never touch
And their eyes look everywhere but each other

Reality comes in the form of a gun fight
The first shots shattered a plate
The second threw gravel as they sped away

The third came in closed door sobs
The fourth is a nuclear bomb
Dropped right into your heart

They both have a story to tell you
When the smoke clears
But it doesn't matter
They're both wrong
All you can see is the ruins of your life
Torn apart by the very people that built it up

That's where the dream ends every night
Watching the war unfold again and again
Unable to change a single moment
Unable to protect the little girl
I barely recognize anymore

10. Window

When I was too young to go out at night
I would fall asleep by the window
Waiting for you to come home

And when I finally got old enough to go
I would fall asleep with my head against the
Passenger window
Too tired, wet, and cold to care if it hurt

And when you left I spent all night
looking out the window
waiting for your sick game to end
waiting for you to come back
and lecture us about whatever we had done
to make you leave this time
but you never came back

Now I fall asleep facing the wall
Nothing good ever comes
From sleeping by the window

11. Survive

How can I explain this to you?
This pain I carry around keeps me safe.
Like a treasured toy, I've had it since childhood.
These are the tricks I learned to survive.
Like a carnival treasure chest
I can reach into whenever someone else is hurting.
Head down,
Quick to laugh,
A pocket full of jokes,
Fast feet,
And a quiet voice.
I am no one.
A spy in the night.
A little girl who learned too young
The world likes you better if you are moldable,
Like play dough.
So that's what I became.
I was a blank page and I let others color me however they wanted.
I smiled through my blood-soaked teeth,
As I clamped down on my tongue
to keep my own voice from coming out.
Now that I've grown,
I still play dress up with everyone else.

Being whatever, they need me to be to stay happy.
I just wish someone would've told me
when you use paint to hide yourself
Eventually it starts to stain.
My skin is a patchwork of stories and lies,
and I can't tell which ones are mine anymore.

12. Good-Morning

My phone buzzed early in the morning.
"Good-morning sweetie have a great day"
But I'd been up for hours already,
and though you were the first to say it,
you were the last person I wanted to hear it from.
So I stare at it in the silence of an empty barn,
wondering if I should type something back.
I stare so long tears form in my eyes
and don't know if they're angry or sad.
Maybe it's just my phones light.
"Morning. Have a great day too"
I send it without meaning a word of it,
wondering as I turn back to work,
if you meant yours.

13. Love and Hate

You loved me when I was useful
And when I thought the world of you
You love me now that I'm the only one
who answers the phone

You hated me when I spoke out of turn
And when I voiced a different opinion
You hate me now that I left the world
You built behind

I wish I could say I hated you for
Forcing me to be someone else
To earn your love
But I never truly learned that lesson

14. Voicemail

It’s a very odd feeling,
you always answer the phone when I call,
but you only ask the same four questions.
And you only tell me the same four details
about your new life.
Yet that call fills me with a guilt that isn’t my own.
While your voice is tinged with a sadness
we both know you don’t mean.
I think its best if we just,
leave each other voicemails from now on.
I can stop replaying this game,
and you can find a new piece to play

15. Miss Me

Sometimes I wonder if you miss me.
Other times I wonder if you even notice I'm gone.
And I can't decide which one hurts worse.

16. Child of Before

I wonder if I'll ever get to see her again
The little girl I was before
I try to tempt her out with
Trips to the movies with an extra-large slushie
Coloring books and stuffed animals
She smiles and takes it all in
We laugh together for a little while
Then she's gone again
Hidden behind her cardboard armor
Weak, old, covered in creases and water damage
But strong enough to keep the world out
Unfortunately, that also means
she keeps herself from the world
I wish there was some way I could show her
it was safe again
Maybe one day I'll be able to convince her to stay
For now, I'll just keep inviting her out
a little more each day
Maybe she still likes cookie dough

17. Rebuild

Child, I want you to listen to me closely.
There is going to be many people
that walk into your heart.
They will make themselves right at home.
You will give them everything you have,
and they will give you all the love you could desire.
But one day they will leave.
They might walk out of your heart
in the middle of the night
without one word of parting.
Leaving you to wake up alone
in a place built for two.
They might try to make it better with words
as they take back everything they gave to you,
and shuffle towards the door.
Others will trash your heart on the way out.
Screaming and throwing things across the room.
Intentionally ruining the place
you both so lovingly built.
I wish I could tell you it only happens once.
That you will find you never really loved them at all.
But I can't.
You will love each one of them wholly,
and they will all leave a mark on your heart

nothing can erase.
When they leave you though,
you must promise me something.
You will rebuild yourself first.
You will not seek out a temporary fix,
fill your heart with violent substances,
to momentarily blind yourself to the pain.
You will grieve for the damage inflicted upon you.
You will mourn for all the dreams that you must let go.
And, when you are ready,
you will pick yourself back up.

18. Stranger in the Mirror

Today I met a stranger in the mirror.
Her hair was dull and frizzy.
Her eyes looked dead,
dark circles clung to them.
Her shoulders sagged
like she'd been carrying too much.
She had a wall built up around her.
But behind that wall was a broken city.
Crumbling ruins turning to dust.

I had watched her lose herself.
It had been slow at first.
But soon the invading army had destroyed
what little defenses she had.
They left a hollow,
empty mask of a girl.
Today though,
I decided I had watched enough.
I would be her revolution.
I would fight for her.

I bathed her in Epsom salts
and jasmine oil.
I dried her in her favorite fluffy towel,

and didn't judge as sobs racked her body.
I conditioned her dry skin,
and brushed her long-tangled hair.
I painted and filed the nails she had chewed on,
and sprayed her wrists with floral perfume.

I helped her into a dress
she forgot she had.
I helped her with her shoes,
handed her a jacket,
and watched her cracked lips form a smile.
Together we called a cab,
To take us to dinner.
I treated her to a movie after.
She was quiet.
But she smiled,
and laughed a little more.
I could see the city start to rebuild.

I made sure she got home safe.
And when she changed into her pajamas,
and looked in the mirror again,
I wasn't a stranger anymore.

19. Forgivness

You didn't deserve an apology,
but I gave you one anyway.

Because while I only cross your mind
when things are going wrong
and you need me to fix them,
I think about you everyday

I had to forgive you
so I could forgive myself
for loving you;
and find some peace
at night.

20. To Whom it May Concern

To whom it may concern,
Know that I no longer flinch
when you call.
Know that the thought of you
doesn't make my heartbeat faster.
Know that I do miss you but,
not who you were rather,
who you could've been.
Know that I am proud of
the person you made me into.
Know that I still hear your voice
when I don't feel strong.
Know that just because you can't
be in my life every day
doesn't mean I still hate you.
Know that I do love you,
always and forever.

Sincerely,
Your little girl

21. Exist Again

I found a place to exist
A place I can be me
Where it's just me
I can go to bed early
And sleep through the night
Without the lights guilting me awake
I can wake up early
And walk downstairs for tea
Without tiptoeing around someone's wrath
I can make dinner for one
A salad when I need it
And sushi when I feel like it
I found a place to exist
A place I can flourish in
where my quiet rituals can be done in peace
Rather than with the whispers of discouragement
Where I can collect beautiful things
Without fearing there will be an accident
Where I can loudly fall in love with life again
Rather than acting uninterested
I found a place to exist
A place I can be me
Where it's just me
And that's okay